—Lyric Booklet—

All the Words to All the Songs in

MERRY CHRISTMAS SONGBOOK

A Reader's Digest Book

Copyright © 2007 The Reader's Digest Association, Inc.

Copyright © 2007 The Reader's Digest Association (Canada) Ltd.

ISBN 978-0-7621-0868-8

We are committed to both the quality of our products and the service we provide to our customers.
We value your comments, so please feel free to contact us:

The Reader's Digest Association, Inc.
Adult Trade Publishing
Reader's Digest Road
Pleasantville, NY 10570-7000

Printed in China
1 3 5 7 9 10 8 6 4 2

Reader's Digest

The Reader's Digest Association, Inc.
Pleasantville, New York / Montreal

SECTION 1
Our Best-Loved Carols

Silent Night

*English words adapted from the original German of
Joseph Mohr; Music by Franz Gruber*

Silent night, holy night,
All is calm, all is bright.
Round yon Virgin Mother and Child,
Holy Infant so tender and mild,
Sleep in heavenly peace;
Sleep in heavenly peace.

Silent night, holy night,
Shepherds quake at the sight.
Glories stream from heaven afar,
Heav'nly hosts sing Alleluia;
Christ the Savior is born;
Christ the Savior is born.

Silent night, holy night,
Son of God, love's pure light.
Radiant beams from Thy holy face,
With the dawn of redeeming grace,
Jesus, Lord, at Thy birth;
Jesus, Lord, at Thy birth.

God Rest Ye Merry, Gentlemen

Traditional

God rest ye merry, gentlemen; let nothing you dismay.
Remember, Christ our Savior was born on Christmas Day
To save us all from Satan's pow'r when we were gone
   astray.

CHORUS
O tidings of comfort and joy, comfort and joy!
O tidings of comfort and joy!

In Bethlehem, in Israel, this blessed Babe was born,
And laid within a manger upon this blessed morn;
The which His Mother Mary did nothing take in scorn.
CHORUS

From God our heav'nly Father, a blessed angel came;
And unto certain shepherds brought tidings of the same;
How that in Bethlehem was born the Son of God by name.
CHORUS

Hark! the Herald Angels Sing

Words by Charles Wesley; Music by Felix Mendelssohn

Hark! the herald angels sing,
"Glory to the newborn King!
Peace on earth and mercy mild,
God and sinners reconciled."
Joyful, all ye nations rise,
Join the triumph of the skies;
With the angelic host proclaim,
"Christ is born in Bethlehem!"

CHORUS
Hark, the herald angels sing,
"Glory to the newborn King!"

Christ by highest heav'n adored;
Christ the everlasting Lord!
Late in time behold Him come,
Offspring of a Virgin's womb.
Veiled in flesh the Godhead see;
Hail the incarnate Deity.
Pleased as man with man to dwell,
Jesus, our Emmanuel!
CHORUS

Hail the heav'n-born Prince of Peace!
Hail the Son of Righteousness!
Light and life to all He brings,
Ris'n with healing in His wings.
Mild He lays His glory by,
Born that man no more may die.
Born to raise the sons of earth;
Born to give them second birth.
CHORUS

O Little Town of Bethlehem

Words by Phillips Brooks; Music by Lewis H. Redner

O little town of Bethlehem,
How still we see thee lie;
Above thy deep and dreamless sleep,
The silent stars go by.
Yet in thy dark streets shineth
The everlasting Light;
The hopes and fears of all the years
Are met in thee tonight.

For Christ is born of Mary,
And gather'd all above,
While mortals sleep, the angels keep
Their watch of wond'ring love.
O morning stars together
Proclaim the holy birth,
And praises sing to God the King
And peace to men on earth.

O holy Child of Bethlehem,
Descend to us, we pray;
Cast out our sin and enter in;
Be born to us today.
We hear the Christmas angels,
The great glad tidings tell;
O come to us, abide with us,
Our Lord Emmanuel.

Deck the Halls

Old Welsh Air

Deck the halls with boughs of holly,
Fa la la la la la la la la.
'Tis the season to be jolly,
Fa la la la la la la la la.
Don we now our gay apparel,
Fa la, fa la la la la.
Troll the ancient Yuletide carol,
Fa la la la la la la la la.

See the blazing Yule before us,
Fa la la la la la la la la.
Strike the harp and join the chorus,
Fa la la la la la la la la.
Follow me in merry measure,
Fa la, fa la la la la.
While I tell of Yuletide treasure,
Fa la la la la la la la la.

We Three Kings of Orient Are

Words and Music by John Henry Hopkins

We three kings of Orient are,
Bearing gifts we traverse afar,
Field and fountain, moor and mountain,
Following yonder star.

CHORUS
O Star of wonder, Star of night,
Star with royal beauty bright,
Westward leading, still proceeding,
Guide us to Thy perfect light.

Born a King on Bethlehem's plain,
Gold I bring to crown Him again,
King forever, ceasing never,
Over us all to reign.
CHORUS

Frankincense to offer have I,
Incense owns a Deity nigh.
Pray'r and praising, all men raising,
Worship Him, God most high.
CHORUS

Myrrh is mine, its bitter perfume
Breathes of life of gathering gloom;
Sorrowing, sighing, bleeding, dying,
Sealed in the stone-cold tomb.
CHORUS

Glorious now behold Him arise,
King and God and Sacrifice.
Alleluia, Alleluia,
Earth to heav'n replies.
CHORUS

O Christmas Tree (O Tannenbaum)

Traditional

O Christmas tree, O Christmas tree, thy leaves are so
    unchanging.
O Christmas tree, O Christmas tree, thy leaves are so
    unchanging.
Not only green when summer's here, but also when 'tis cold
    and drear.
O Christmas tree, O Christmas tree, thy leaves are so
    unchanging.

O Christmas tree, O Christmas tree, you fill all hearts with
    gaiety.
O Christmas tree, O Christmas tree, you fill all hearts with
    gaiety.
On Christmas Day you stand so tall, affording joy to one and
    all.
O Christmas tree, O Christmas tree, you fill all hearts with
    gaiety.

O Tannenbaum, O Tannenbaum, wie treu sind deine Blätter.
O Tannenbaum, O Tannenbaum, wie treu sind deine Blätter.
Du grünst nicht nur zur Sommerzeit, nein auch im Winter
    wenn es schneit.
O Tannenbaum, O Tannenbaum, wie treu sind deine Blätter.

It Came Upon the Midnight Clear

Words by Edmund Hamilton Sears; Music by Richard Storrs Willis

It came upon the midnight clear
That glorious song of old,
From angels bending near the earth
To touch their harps of gold.
"Peace on the earth, goodwill to men,
From heav'n's all-gracious King."
The world in solemn stillness lay
To hear the angels sing.

Still through the cloven skies they come
With peaceful wings unfurl'd;
And still their heav'nly music floats

(continued on next page)

O'er all the weary world.
Above its sad and lowly plains,
They bend on hov'ring wing;
And ever o'er its Babel sounds
The blessed angels sing.

For lo! the days are hast'ning on,
By prophets seen of old,
When with the ever-circling years
Shall come the time foretold.
When the new heav'n and earth shall own
The Prince of Peace, their King,
And the whole of world send back the song
Which now the angels sing.

Joy to the World

Words by Isaac Watts; Music by Lowell Mason

Joy to the world! the Lord has come:
Let earth receive her King.
Let ev'ry heart prepare Him room,
And heav'n and nature sing, and heav'n and nature sing,
And heav'n, and heav'n and nature sing.

Joy to the world! the Savior reigns:
Let men their songs employ,
While fields and floods, rocks, hills and plains
Repeat the sounding joy, repeat the sounding joy,
Repeat, repeat the sounding joy.

He rules the world with truth and grace,
And makes the nations prove
The glories of His righteousness
And wonders of His love, and wonders of His love,
And wonders, wonders of His love.

The First Noël

Traditional

The first Noël, the angel did say,
Was to certain poor shepherds in fields as they lay;
In fields where they lay keeping their sheep,
On a cold winter's night that was so deep.

CHORUS
Noël, Noël, Noël, Noël,
Born is the King of Israel.

They looked up and saw a star,
Shining in the East beyond them far;
And to the earth it gave great light,
And so it continued day and night.
CHORUS

This star drew nigh to the northwest;
O'er Bethlehem it took its rest,
And there it did both stop and stay,
Right o'er the place where Jesus lay.
CHORUS

O Come, All Ye Faithful (Adeste Fideles)

*English words by Frederick Oakeley; Latin words
attributed to John Francis Wade;
Music by John Reading*

O come, all ye faithful,
Joyful and triumphant,
O come ye, O come ye to Bethlehem.
Come and behold Him, born the King of angels.

CHORUS
O come, let us adore Him,
O come, let us adore Him,
O come, let us adore Him,
Christ, the Lord.

Sing, choirs of angels,
Sing in exultation;
Sing all ye citizens of heav'n above:
Glory to God in the Highest.
CHORUS

Yea, Lord, we greet Thee,
Born this happy morning;
Jesus, to Thee be glory giv'n;
Word of the Father, now in flesh appearing.
CHORUS

*Adeste fideles,
Laeti triumphantes,
Venite, venite in Bethlehem.
Natum videte, Regem angelorum.
Venite adoremus;
Venite adoremus;
Venite adoremus, Dominum.*

The Twelve Days of Christmas

Traditional

On the first day of Christmas, my true love sent to me
A partridge in a pear tree.

On the second day of Christmas, my true love sent to me
Two turtle doves and a partridge in a pear tree.

On the third day of Christmas, my true love sent to me
Three French hens, two turtle doves
And a partridge in a pear tree.

On the fourth day of Christmas, my true love sent to me
Four calling birds, three French hens, two turtle doves
And a partridge in a pear tree.

On the fifth day of Christmas, my true love sent to me
Five golden rings.
Four calling birds, three French hens, two turtle doves
And a partridge in a pear tree.

On the sixth day of Christmas, my true love gave to me
Six geese a-laying,
Five golden rings.
Four calling birds, three French hens, two turtle doves
And a partridge in a pear tree.

On the seventh day of Christmas, my true love gave to me
Seven swans a-swimming, six geese a-laying,
Five golden rings.
Four calling birds, three French hens, two turtle doves
And a partridge in a pear tree.

On the eighth day of Christmas, my true love gave to me
Eight maids a-milking, seven swans a-swimming, six geese
   a-laying,
Five golden rings.
Four calling birds, three French hens, two turtle doves
And a partridge in a pear tree.

On the ninth day of Christmas, my true love gave to me
Nine ladies dancing, eight maids a-milking, seven swans
   a-swimming, six geese a-laying,
Five golden rings.
Four calling birds, three French hens, two turtle doves
And a partridge in a pear tree.

On the tenth day of Christmas, my true love gave to me
Ten lords a-leaping, nine ladies dancing, eight maids
   a-milking, seven swans a-swimming, six geese a-laying,
Five golden rings.
Four calling birds, three French hens, two turtle doves
And a partridge in a pear tree.

On the eleventh day of Christmas, my true love gave to me
Eleven pipers piping, ten lords a-leaping, nine ladies
   dancing, eight maids a-milking, seven swans
   a-swimming, six geese a-laying,
Five golden rings.
Four calling birds, three French hens, two turtle doves
And a partridge in a pear tree.

On the twelfth day of Christmas, my true love gave to me
Twelve drummers drumming, eleven pipers piping, ten lords
   a-leaping, nine ladies dancing, eight maids a-milking,
   seven swans a-swimming, six geese a-laying,
Five golden rings.
Four calling birds, three French hens, two turtle doves
And a partridge in a pear tree.

Away in a Manger

Traditional

Away in a manger, no crib for a bed,
The little Lord Jesus laid down His sweet head.
The stars in the sky looked down where He lay,
The little Lord Jesus asleep on the hay.

The cattle are lowing, the poor Baby wakes,
But little Lord Jesus no crying He makes.
I love Thee, Lord Jesus, look down from the sky,
And stay by my cradle till morning is nigh.

Be near me, Lord Jesus, I ask Thee to stay
Close by me forever and love me I pray.
Bless all the dear children in Thy tender care,
And take us to heaven to live with Thee there.

Angels We Have Heard on High

Traditional

Angels we have heard on high
Sweetly singing o'er the plains,
And the mountains in reply
Echoing their joyous strains.

CHORUS
Gloria in excelsis Deo,
Gloria in excelsis Deo.

Shepherds, why this jubilee?
Why your joyous strains prolong?
What the gladsome tidings be
Which inspire your heav'nly song?
CHORUS

Come to Bethlehem and see
Him whose birth the angels sing.
Come adore on bended knee
Christ the Lord, the newborn King.
CHORUS

Good King Wenceslas

Words by John Mason Neal; Music Traditional

Good King Wenceslas look'd out on the feast of Stephen,
When the snow lay round about, deep and crisp and even.
Brightly shone the moon that night, though the frost was
   cruel,
When a poor man came in sight, gath'ring winter fuel.

"Hither, page, and stand by me, if thou know'st it, telling,
Yonder peasant, who is he? Where and what his dwelling?"
"Sire, he lives a good league hence, underneath the
   mountain;
Right against the forest fence, by Saint Agnes' fountain."

5

(continued on next page)

"Bring me flesh and bring me wine, bring me pine logs
hither.
Thou and I will see him dine, when we bear him thither."
Page and monarch forth they went, forth they went
together,
Through the rude wind's wild lament and the bitter weather.

"Sire, the night is darker now, and the wind blows stronger.
Fails my heart, I know not how, I can go no longer."
"Mark my footsteps, my good page, tread thou in them
boldly.
Thou shalt find the winter's rage freeze thy blood less
coldly."

In his master's steps he trod, where the snow lay dinted.
Heat was in the very sod which the Saint had printed.
Therefore, Christian men, be sure, wealth or rank
possessing;
Ye who now will bless the poor shall yourselves find
blessing.

Here We Come A-Caroling (The Wassail Song)

Traditional

Here we come a-caroling among the leaves so green;
Here we come a-wand'ring so fair to be seen.

CHORUS
Love and joy come to you,
And to you glad Christmas too,
And God bless you and send you a Happy New Year,
And God send you a Happy New Year.

We are not daily beggars that beg from door to door,
But we are neighbors' children whom you have seen
before.
CHORUS

God bless the master of this house, likewise the mistress
too,
And all the little children that round the table go
CHORUS

We Wish You a Merry Christmas

Traditional

We wish you a Merry Christmas;
We wish you a Merry Christmas;
We wish you a Merry Christmas and a Happy New Year.

CHORUS
Good tidings to you wherever you are;
Good tidings for Christmas and a Happy New Year.

Oh, bring us a figgy pudding;
Oh, bring us a figgy pudding;

Oh, bring us a figgy pudding and a cup of good cheer.
CHORUS

We won't go until we've got some;
We won't go until we've got some;
We won't go until we've got some, so bring some out here.
CHORUS

We wish you a Merry Christmas;
We wish you a Merry Christmas;
We wish you a Merry Christmas and a Happy New Year.
CHORUS

SECTION 2
Popular Christmas Hits

The Christmas Song
(Chestnuts Roasting on an Open Fire)

Lyric and Music by Mel Tormé and Robert Wells

Chestnuts roasting on an open fire,
Jack Frost nipping at your nose,
Yuletide carols being sung by a choir
And folks dressed up like Eskimos.
Ev'rybody knows a turkey and some mistletoe
Help to make the season bright.
Tiny tots with their eyes all aglow
Will find it hard to sleep tonight.
They know that Santa's on his way;
He's loaded lots of toys and goodies on his sleigh.
And ev'ry mother's child is gonna spy
To see if reindeer really know how to fly.
And so I'm offering this simple phrase
To kids from one to ninety-two;
Although it's been said many times, many ways,
"Merry Christmas to you."

Have Yourself a Merry Little Christmas

Words and Music by Hugh Martin and Ralph Blane

Have yourself a merry little Christmas;
Let your heart be light.
From now on, our troubles will be out of sight.
Have yourself a merry little Christmas;
Make the Yuletide gay.

From now on, our troubles will be miles away.
Here we are as in olden days, happy golden days of yore;
Faithful friends who are dear to us gather near to us once
    more.
Through the years we all will be together
If the Fates allow.
Hang a shining star upon the highest bough,
And have yourself a merry little Christmas now.

I'll Be Home for Christmas

Words by Kim Gannon; Music by Walter Kent

I'll be home for Christmas;
You can plan on me.
Please have snow and mistletoe
And presents on the tree.
Christmas Eve will find me
Where the love-light gleams.
I'll be home for Christmas
If only in my dreams.

Christmas in Killarney

*Words and Music by John Redmond,
James Cavanaugh and Frank Weldon*

The holly green, the ivy green,
The prettiest picture you've ever seen
Is Christmas in Killarney
With all of the folks at home.
It's nice, you know, to kiss your beau
While cuddling under the mistletoe,
And Santa Claus you know, of course,
Is one of the boys from home.
The door is always open;
The neighbors pay a call;
And Father John before he's gone
Will bless the house and all.
How grand it feels to click your heels
And join in the fun of the jigs and reels;
I'm handing you no blarney,
The likes you've never known
Is Christmas in Killarney
With all of the folks at home.

The Merry Christmas Polka

Words by Paul Francis Webster; Music by Sonny Burke

They're tuning up the fiddles now, the fiddles now, the
    fiddles now;

There's wine to warm the middles now and set your head
    awhirl.
Around and round the room we go, the room we go, the
    room we go;
Around and round the room we go, so get yourself a girl.
Now ev'ry heart will start to tingle,
When sleigh bells jingle on Santa's sleigh;
Together we will greet Kris Kringle
And another Christmas Day.
Come on and dance the merry Christmas polka;
Let ev'ryone be happy and gay.
Oh, it's the time to be jolly and deck the halls with holly;
So let's have a jolly holiday.
Come on and dance the merry Christmas polka;
Another joyous season has begun.
Roll out the Yuletide barrels and sing out the carols,
A merry Christmas ev'ryone!
Come on and dance the merry Christmas polka;
Let ev'ry lady step with her beau
Around a tree to the ceiling with lots of time for stealing
Those kisses beneath the mistletoe.
Come on and dance the merry Christmas polka,
With ev'rybody joining in the fun;
Roll out the barrels that cheer you, and shout till they hear
    you,
A merry Christmas ev'ryone!

Blue Christmas

Words and Music by Billy Hayes and Jay Johnson

I'll have a blue Christmas without you;
I'll be so blue thinking about you.
Decorations of red on a green Christmas tree
Won't mean a thing if you're not here with me.
I'll have a blue Christmas, that's certain;
And when that blue heartache starts hurtin',
You'll be doin' all right with your Christmas of white,
But I'll have a blue, blue Christmas.

We Need a Little Christmas

Music and Lyric by Jerry Herman

Haul out the holly;
Put up the tree before my spirit falls again.
Fill up the stocking,
I may be rushing things, but deck the halls again now.
For we need a little Christmas
Right this very minute,
Candles in the window,
Carols at the spinet.
Yes, we need a little Christmas

(continued on next page)

Right this very minute.
It hasn't snowed a single flurry,
But Santa, dear, we're in a hurry;
So climb down the chimney;
Turn on the brightest string of light I've ever seen.
Slice up the fruitcake;
It's time we hung some tinsel on that evergreen bough.
For I've grown a little leaner,
Grown a little colder,
Grown a little sadder,
Grown a little older,
And I need a little angel
Sitting on my shoulder,
Need a little Christmas now.
For we need a little music,
Need a little laughter,
Need a little singing
Ringing through the rafter,
And we need a little snappy
"Happy ever after,"
Need a little Christmas now.

The Little Boy That Santa Claus Forgot

Words and Music by Tommie Connor,
Jimmy Leach and Michael Carr

Christmas comes but once a year for ev'ry girl and boy,
The laughter and the joy they find in each toy.
I'll tell you of a little boy who lives across the way;
This little feller's Christmas is just another day.
He's the little boy that Santa Claus forgot,
And goodness knows he didn't want a lot.
He sent a note to Santa for some soldiers and a drum;
It broke his little heart when he found Santa hadn't come.
In the street, he envies all those lucky boys,
Then wanders home to last year's broken toys.
I'm so sorry for that laddie;
He hasn't got a daddy,
The little boy that Santa Claus forgot.

Christmas for Cowboys

Words and Music by Steve Weisberg

Tall in the saddle we spend Christmas Day,
Drivin' the cattle on the snow-covered plains.
All of the good gifts given today;
Ours is the sky and the wide open range.

Back in the cities, they have diff'rent ways,
Football and eggnog and Christmas parades.

I'll take the blanket; I'll take the reins;
Christmas for cowboys and wide open plains.

A campfire for warmth as we stop for the night;
The stars overhead are the Christmas-tree lights.
The wind sings a hymn as we bow down to pray;
Christmas for cowboys and the wide open range.
It's tall in the saddle we spend Christmas Day,
Drivin' the cattle on the snow-covered plains.
So many gifts have been opened today;
Ours is the sky and the wide open range.
It's Christmas for cowboys and wide open plains.

Christmas Is

Words by Spence Maxwell; Music by Percy Faith

Christmas is sleigh bells;
Christmas is sharing;
Christmas is holly;
Christmas is caring.
Christmas is children who just can't go to sleep.
Christmas is mem'ries, the kind you always keep.
Deck the halls and give a cheer
For all the things that Christmas is each year.
Christmas, merry Christmas,
When all your wishes come true.

Christmas is carols to warm you in the snow;
Christmas is bedtime where no one wants to go.
All the world is tinsel bright,
So glad to know that Christmas is tonight.
Christmas, merry Christmas,
When all your wishes come true,
Christmas, merry Christmas;
May all your wishes come true.

Welcome Christmas
(*From* "How the Grinch Stole Christmas")

Music by Albert Hague; Lyrics by Dr. Seuss

Fah who foraze! Dah who doraze!
Welcome Christmas, Come this way!
Fah who foraze! Dah who doraze!
Welcome Christmas, Christmas Day!

Welcome, welcome! Fah who ramus!
Welcome, welcome! Dah who dahmus,
Christmas Day is in our grasp!
So long as we have hands to clasp!

Fah who foraze! Dah who doraze!
Welcome Christmas! Bring your cheer.

Fah who foraze! Dah who doraze!
Welcome all who's far and near.

Fah who foraze! Dah who doraze!
Welcome Christmas, Come this way!
Fah who foraze! Dah who doraze!
Welcome Christmas, Christmas Day!

Welcome, Christmas! Fah who ramus!
Welcome, Christmas! Dah who dahmus,
Christmas Day will always be
Just as long as we have we!

Fah who foraze! Dah who doraze!
Welcome Christmas! Bring your cheer.
Fah who foraze! Dah who doraze!
Welcome all who's far and near.

Take Me Back to Toyland

Words by Kal Mann; Music by Bernie Lowe

Please take me back to Toyland;
Ev'ryone's happy there.
It's more than a girl and boy land
Where dreams just like toys can be shared.
If you believe in Toyland,
Believe in things that you cannot see;
All the world would become a joyland;
What a wonderful world this would be.

C-H-R-I-S-T-M-A-S

Words by Jenny Lou Carson; Music by Eddy Arnold

When I was but a youngster, Christmas meant one thing,
That I'd be getting lots of toys that day.
I learned a whole lot diff'rent when Mother sat me down
And taught me to spell Christmas this way:
"C" is for the Christ Child born upon this day;
"H" for herald angels in the night.
"R" means our Redeemer; "I" means Israel;
"S" is for the star that shone so bright.
"T" is for three wise men,
They who traveled far.
"M" is for the manger where He lay.
"A" is for all He stands for;
"S" means shepherds came,
And that's why there's a Christmas Day.

That's What I Want for Christmas

Words by Irving Caesar; Music by Gerald Marks

Make my mommy's life a song;
Keep my daddy safe and strong;
Let me have them all year long;
That's what I want for Christmas.
Let my dolls be made of rags,
Fireman hats of paper bags.
Just write "love" on the Christmas tags;
That's what I want for Christmas
When I wake up Christmas Day,
I would like to find a sleigh;
But if I don't, dear Santa Claus,
I will not complain because
What I really want is this:
Sister's smile and brother's kiss.
Fill our land with peace and bliss
From Maine down to the Isthmus;
That's what I want for Christmas.
I don't want electric trains,
Twenty-dollar aeroplanes.
Free our friends of aches and pains;
That's what I want for Christmas.
I like boots with tops of blue
Like my little sisters do;
So, if you leave them, leave a few;
That's what I want for Christmas.
When the reindeer pass my house,
I'll be quiet as a mouse.
But, when I wake up, let me see
Marching round the Christmas tree
Animals that never bite,
Never giving any fright,
Soldier boys who never fight;
That's what I want for Christmas.
Yes, that's what I want for Christmas.

Will Santy Come to Shanty Town?

Words and Music by Eddy Arnold, Steve Nelson and Ed Nelson, Jr.

Will Santy Come to Shanty Town to a poor little boy like me?
Will he bring me some toys like the other girls and boys?
Will Santy come to Shanty Town if he sees our Christmas
 tree?
Mommy said he would if I promised to be good.
For we don't have a fireplace or a chimney on our shack
Like the other lucky children who live across the track.
Now, if I say my pray'rs each day, when Christmas rolls
 around,
Will Santy come to Shanty Town?

Will Santy come to Shanty Town to a poor little boy like me?
Will he bring me some toys like the other girls and boys?
Will Santy come to Shanty Town if he sees our Christmas
 tree?
Mommy said he would if I promised to be good.
He didn't stop last Christmas Eve; doesn't he know we live
 here?
Will my mommy have to paint my toys the way she did last
 year?
Now, if I say my pray'rs each day, when Christmas rolls
 around,
Will Santy come to Shanty Town?

Rockin' Around the Christmas Tree

Words and Music by Johnny Marks

Rockin' around the Christmas tree
At the Christmas party hop.
Mistletoe hung where you can see
Ev'ry couple tries to stop.
Rockin' around the Christmas tree,
Let the Christmas spirit ring.
Later we'll have some pumpkin pie,
And we'll do some caroling
You will get a sentimental feeling
When you hear voices singing,
"Let's be jolly;
Deck the halls with boughs of holly."
Rockin' around the Christmas tree,
Have a happy holiday.
Ev'ryone dancing merrily
In the new old-fashioned way.

The Christmas Waltz

Words by Sammy Cahn; Music by Jule Styne

Frosted window panes, candles gleaming inside,
Painted candy canes on the tree;
Santa's on his way,
He's filled his sleigh with things, things for you and for me.
It's that time of year,
When the world falls in love,
Ev'ry song you hear seems to say:
"Merry Christmas, may your New Year dreams come true."
And this song of mine,
In three-quarter time,
Wishes you and yours the same thing too.

SECTION 3
For Children
at Christmastime

Rudolph the Red-Nosed Reindeer

Words and Music by Johnny Marks

You know Dasher and Dancer and Prancer and Vixen,
Comet and Cupid and Donner and Blitzen,
But do you recall
The most famous reindeer of all?
Rudolph the Red-Nosed Reindeer
Had a very shiny nose,
And if you ever saw it,
You could even say it glows.
All of the other reindeer
Used to laugh and call him names;
They never let poor Rudolph
Join in any reindeer games.
Then one foggy Christmas Eve,
Santa came to say:
"Rudolph with your nose so bright,
Won't you guide my sleigh tonight?"
Then how the reindeer loved him
As they shouted out with glee,
"Rudolph the Red-Nosed Reindeer,
You'll go down in history."

Thirty-Two Feet and Eight Little Tails

Words and Music by John Redmond, James Cavanaugh, and Frank Weldon

Dasher, Dancer, Prancer, Vixen,
Comet, Cupid, Donner, Blitzen,
Over the moon so bright,
Thirty-two feet and eight little tails of white,
Hurry, hurry, hurry through the night.

Ol' Saint Nick, he works so quickly,
Leaving toys for girls and boys.
Then over the roofs so high,
Thirty-two feet and eight little tails they fly,
Faster, faster, faster through the sky.
Ohhh! look at 'em go;
Santa's laughin', ho, ho, ho, ho, ho, ho, ho, ho, ho!

Dasher, Dancer, Prancer, Vixen,
Comet, Cupid, Donner, Blitzen,
Over the garden wall,
Thirty-two feet and eight little tails in all.
See them canter, hear old Santa call:
"Merry, Merry Christmas to you,
Merry, Merry Christmas to you all."

Here Comes Santa Claus

Words and Music by Gene Autry and Oakley Haldeman

Here Comes Santa Claus, here comes Santa Claus
Right down Santa Claus Lane.
Vixen and Blitzen and all his reindeer are pulling on the rein.
Bells are ringing, children singing;
All is merry and bright.
Hang your stockings and say your pray'rs,
'Cause Santa Claus comes tonight.

Here Comes Santa Claus, here comes Santa Claus
Right down Santa Claus Lane.
He's got a bag that is filled with toys for the girls and boys
    again.
Hear those sleigh bells jingle jangle,
What a beautiful sight.
Jump in bed, cover up your head,
'Cause Santa Claus comes tonight.

Here Comes Santa Claus, here comes Santa Claus
Right down Santa Claus Lane.
He doesn't care if you're rich or poor for he loves you just
    the same.
Santa knows that we're God's children;
That makes ev'rything right.
Fill your hearts with a Christmas cheer,
'Cause Santa Claus comes tonight.

Here Comes Santa Claus, here comes Santa Claus
Right down Santa Claus Lane.
He'll come around when the chimes ring out; then it's
    Christmas morn again.
Peace on earth will come to all
If we just follow the light.
Let's give thanks to the Lord above,
'Cause Santa Claus comes tonight.

Santa Claus Is Comin' to Town

Words and Music by J. Fred Coots and Haven Gillespie

You better watch out; you better not cry;
Better not pout; I'm telling you why:
Santa Claus is comin' to town.
He's making a list and checking it twice;
Gonna find out who's naughty and nice:
Santa Claus is comin' to town.
He sees you when you're sleepin';
He knows when you're awake;
He knows if you've been bad or good;
So be good for goodness sake.
Oh! You better watch out; you better not cry;
Better not pout; I'm telling you why;
Santa Claus is comin' to town.

A Holly Jolly Christmas

Words and Music by Johnny Marks

Have a holly jolly Christmas;
It's the best time of the year.
I don't know if there'll be snow, but have a cup of cheer.
Have a holly jolly Christmas,
And when you walk down the street,
Say hello to friends you know and ev'ryone you meet.
Oh, ho, the mistletoe hung where you can see;
Somebody waits for you;
Kiss her once for me.
Have a holly jolly Christmas, and in case you didn't hear,
Oh, by golly, have a holly jolly Christmas this year.
Oh, ho, the mistletoe hung where you can see;
Somebody waits for you;
Kiss her once for me.
Have a holly jolly Christmas, and in case you didn't hear,
Oh, by golly, have a holly jolly Christmas this year.

When Santa Claus Gets Your Letter

Words and Music by Johnny Marks

When Santa Claus gets your letter, you know what he will
   say:
"Have you been good the way you should on ev'ry single
   day?"
When Santa Claus gets your letter to ask for Christmas
   toys,
He'll take a look in his good book he keeps for girls and
   boys.
He'll stroke his beard, his eyes will glow, and at your name
   he'll peer:
It takes a little time, you know, to check back one whole
   year!
When Santa Claus gets your letter, I really do believe,
You'll head his list, you won't be missed, by Santa on
   Christmas Eve.

Up on the Housetop

Words and Music by Benjamin Russell Hanby

Up on the housetop reindeer pause;
Out jumps good old Santa Claus,
Down through the chimney with lots of toys,
All for the little ones' Christmas joys.

CHORUS
Ho, ho, ho who wouldn't go?
Ho, ho, ho who wouldn't go?
Up on the housetop, click, click, click,
Down through the chimney with good Saint Nick.

First comes the stocking of Little Nell;
Oh, dear Santa, fill it well;
Give her a dolly that laughs and cries,
One that can open and shut its eyes.
CHORUS

Look in the stocking of little Bill;
Oh, just see that glorious fill!
Here is a hammer and lots of tacks,
Whistle and ball and a set of jacks.
CHORUS

Frosty the Snow Man

Words and Music by Steve Nelson and Jack Rollins

Frosty the Snow Man was a jolly, happy soul,
With a corncob pipe and a button nose and two eyes made
   out of coal.
Frosty the Snow Man is a fairy tale, they say;
He was made of snow, but the children know how he came
   to life one day.
There must have been some magic in that old silk hat they
   found,
For when they placed it on his head, he began to dance
   around.
Oh, Frosty the Snow Man was alive as he could be,
And the children say he could laugh and play just the same
   as you and me.

Frosty the Snow Man knew the sun was hot that day,
So he said, "Let's run and we'll have some fun now before
   I melt away."
Down to the village with a broomstick in his hand,
Running here and there all around the square, sayin',
   "Catch me if you can."
He led them down the streets of town right to the traffic
   cop,
And he only paused a moment when he heard him holler
   "Stop!"
For Frosty the Snow Man had to hurry on his way,
But he waved good-bye, sayin', "Don't you cry; I'll be back
   again someday."

Thumpety thump thump, thumpety thump thump,
Look at Frosty go;
Thumpety thump thump, thumpety thump thump,
Over the hills of snow.

(All I Want for Christmas Is) My Two Front Teeth

Words and Music by Don Gardner

All I want for Christmas is my two front teeth, my two front
   teeth, see my two front teeth.
Gee, if I could only have my two front teeth,
Then I could wish you "Merry Christmas."
It seems so long since I could say,
"Sister Susie sitting on a thistle."
Gosh, oh gee, how happy I'd be
If I could only whistle.
All I want for Christmas is my two front teeth, my two front
   teeth, see my two front teeth.
Gee, if I could only have my two front teeth,
Then I could wish you "Merry Christmas."

Suzy Snowflake

Words and Music by Sid Tepper and Roy C. Bennett

Here comes Suzy Snowflake,
Dressed in a snow-white gown,
Tap, tap, tappin' at your windowpane
To tell you she's in town.
Here comes Suzy Snowflake;
Soon you will hear her say,
"Come out ev'ryone and play with me;
I haven't long to stay.
If you wanna make a snowman,
I'll help you make one, one, two, three.
If you wanna take a sleigh ride,
The ride's on me."
Here comes Suzy Snowflake;
Look at her tumblin' down,
Bringing joy to ev'ry girl and boy;
Suzy's come to town.

Toyland

Words by Glen MacDonough; Music by Victor Herbert

Toyland, toyland,
Little girl and boy land,
While you dwell within it,
You are ever happy then.
Childhood's joyland,
Mystic, merry Toyland!
Once you pass its borders,
You can ne'er return again.

Nuttin' for Christmas

Words and Music by Sid Tepper and Roy C. Bennett

I broke my bat on Johnny's head;
Somebody snitched on me.
I hid a frog in sister's bed;
Somebody snitched on me.
I spilled some ink on Mommy's rug;
I made Tommy eat a bug;
Brought some gum with a penny slug;
Somebody snitched on me. Oh,

CHORUS
I'm gettin' nuttin' for Christmas;
Mommy and Daddy are mad.
I'm gettin' nuttin' for Christmas,
'Cause I ain't been nuttin' but bad.

I put a tack on teacher's chair;
Somebody snitched on me.
I tied a knot in Susie's hair;
Somebody snitched on me.

I did a dance on Mommy's plants,
Climbed a tree and tore my pants,
Filled the sugar bowl with ants;
Somebody snitched on me. So,
CHORUS

I won't be seeing Santa Claus;
Somebody snitched on me.
He won't come visit me because
Somebody snitched on me.
Next year I'll be going straight;
Next year I'll be good, just wait;
I'd start now, but it's too late;
Somebody snitched on me. Oh,
CHORUS

So you better be good whatever you do,
'Cause if you're bad, I'm warning you,
You'll get nuttin' for Christmas.

The Night Before Christmas Song

Words by Clement Clarke Moore, adapted by Johnny Marks; Music by Johnny Marks

'Twas the night before Christmas and all through the house
Not a creature was stirring, not even a mouse.
All the stockings were hung by the chimney with care
In the hope that Saint Nicholas soon would be there.
Then, what to my wondering eyes should appear,
A miniature sleigh and eight tiny reindeer,
A little old driver so lively and quick,
I knew in a moment it must be Saint Nick.
And more rapid than eagles his reindeer all came
As he shouted, "On, Dasher" and each reindeer's name.
And so up to the housetop the reindeer soon flew
With the sleigh full of toys and Saint Nicholas, too.
Down the chimney he came with a leap and a bound;
He was dressed all in fur, and his belly was round.
He spoke not a word but went straight to his work,
And filled all the stockings, then turned with a jerk.
And laying his finger aside of his nose,
Then giving a nod up the chimney he rose.
But I heard him exclaim as he drove out of sight,
"Merry Christmas to all and to all a good night!"

Santa Claus, Indiana, U.S.A.

Words and Music by Abe Olman and Al Jacobs

I wish my daddy and mommy would take me all the way
To Santa Claus, Indiana, U.S.A.
I'd find the letters for Santa, the ones that went astray,
In Santa Claus, Indiana, U.S.A.
I'd answer good little girls and boys,
Saying Santa will bring your toys.
With eight reindeer he'll appear, riding on a sleigh.
Then I'd mail Daddy's and Mommy's surprise for Christmas
    Day,
From Santa Claus, Indiana, U.S.
Santa Claus, Indiana, U.S.
Santa Claus, Indiana, U.S.A.

Grandma Got Run Over by a Reindeer

Words and Music by Randy Brooks

CHORUS
Grandma got run over by a reindeer
Walking home from our house Christmas Eve.
You can say there's no such thing as Santa,
But as for me and Grandpa, we believe.

She'd been drinking too much eggnog
And we begged her not to go,
But she forgot her medication,
And she staggered out the door into the snow.

When we found her Christmas morning
At the scene of the attack,
She had footprints on her forehead,
And incriminating Claus marks on her back.

Now we're all so proud of Grandpa,
He's been taking this so well.
See him in there watching football,
Drinking beer and playing cards with Cousin Mel.

It's not Christmas without Grandma,
All the family's dressed in black.
And we just can't help but wonder:
Should we open up her gifts or send them back?

Now the goose is on the table,
And the pudding made of fig,
And the blue and silver candles
That would just have matched the hair in Grandma's wig.

I've warned all my friends and neighbors,
Better watch out for yourselves.
They should never give a license
To a man who drives a sleigh and plays with elves.

Happy Birthday, Jesus

Words by Estelle Levitt; Music by Lee Pockriss

Katy got a dolly that cries and blinks its eyes;
Jimmy got an automatic plane that really flies.
But we were poor that Christmas, so Momma stayed up all
    night long,
Sitting in the kitchen making us a present; it was this song:

CHORUS
Church bells ring-a-ling; angels sing-a-ling;
"Happy Birthday, Jesus."
Snowflakes ting-a-ling; sleigh bells jing-a-ling;
"Happy Birthday, Jesus."
All year long we wait just to celebrate this Christmas morn,
'Cause we want You to know we're so glad You were born.
Oh, have a merry, very Happy Birthday, Jesus.

Teddy bears get broken, and trains will rust away;
All the fancy playthings seem to fall apart one day.
But I was very lucky, when ev'rybody's gift was gone,
I still had my present; Momma's song of Christmas lived
    on and on:
CHORUS

Christmas is for children, and now I have my own;
Their eyes are full of wonder when all the toys are shown.
But I'll give them something better than anything that's
    on TV,
Something very special, something made forever, this
    melody:
CHORUS

SECTION 4
Christmas
Is a Winter Festival

It's Beginning to Look Like Christmas

Words and Music by Meredith Willson

It's beginning to look a lot like Christmas
Ev'rywhere you go;
Take a look in the five-and-ten, glistening once again
With candy canes and silver lanes aglow.
It's beginning to look a lot like Christmas,
Toys in ev'ry store,
But the prettiest sight to see is the holly that will be
On your own front door.

A pair of hopalong boots and a pistol that shoots
Is the wish of Barney and Ben;
Dolls that will talk and will go for a walk
Is the hope of Janice and Jen;
And Mom and Dad can hardly wait for school to start again.
It's beginning to look a lot like Christmas
Ev'rywhere you go;
There's a tree in the Grand Hotel, one in the park as well,
The sturdy kind that doesn't mind the snow.
It's beginning to look a lot like Christmas;
Soon the bells will start,
And the thing that will make them ring is the carol that you
    sing
Right within your heart.

Jingle Bells

Words and Music by James Pierpont

Dashing through the snow
In a one-horse open sleigh;
O'er the fields we go,
Laughing all the way.
Bells on bobtail ring,
Making spirits bright;
What fun it is to ride and sing
A sleighing song tonight.
Oh! jingle bells, jingle bells, jingle all the way;
Oh, what fun it is to ride in a one-horse open sleigh.
Hey! jingle bells, jingle bells, jingle all the way;
Oh, what fun it is to ride in a one-horse open sleigh!

Let It Snow! Let It Snow! Let It Snow!

Words by Sammy Cahn; Music by Jule Styne

Oh, the weather outside is frightful,
But the fire is so delightful,
And since we've no place to go,
Let it snow, let it snow, let it snow.
It doesn't show signs of stopping,
And I brought some corn for popping;
The lights are turned way down low,
Let it snow, let it snow, let it snow.
When we finally kiss good night,
How I'll hate going out in the storm;
But if you'll really hold me tight,
All the way home I'll be warm.
The fire is slowly dying,
And, my dear, we're still good-byeing,
But as long as you love me so,
Let it snow, let it snow, let it snow.

A Marshmallow World

Words by Carl Sigman; Music by Peter De Rose

It's a marshmallow world in the winter
When the snow comes to cover the ground.
It's the time for play; it's a whipped-cream day;
I wait for it the whole year round.
Those are marshmallow clouds being friendly
In the arms of the evergreen trees,
And the sun is red like a pumpkin head;
It's shining so your nose won't freeze.
The world is your snowball; see how it grows;
That's how it goes whenever it snows.
The world is your snowball just for a song;
Get out and roll it along.
It's a yum-yummy world made for sweethearts;
Take a walk with your favorite girl.
It's a sugar date; what if spring is late;
In winter, it's a marshmallow world.

Sleigh Ride

Words by Mitchell Parish; Music by Leroy Anderson

Just hear those sleigh bells jingling, ring-ting-tingling, too;
Come on, it's lovely weather for a sleigh ride together with
    you.
Outside, the snow is falling and friends are calling
    "Yoo-hoo";
Come on, it's lovely weather for a sleigh ride together with
    you.
Giddy-yap, giddy-yap, giddy-yap, let's go;
Let's look at the show;
We're riding in a wonderland of snow.
Giddy-yap, giddy-yap, giddy-yap, it's grand,
Just holding your hand;
We're gliding along with a song of a wintery fairyland.
Our cheeks are nice and rosy, and comfy cozy are we;
We're snuggled up together like two birds of a feather
    would be.
Let's take that road before us and sing a chorus or two;
Come on, it's lovely weather for a sleigh ride together with
    you.

Over the River and Through the Woods

Traditional

Over the river and through the woods
To Grandmother's house we go.
The horse knows the way to carry the sleigh
Through white and drifted snow.
Over the river and through the woods,
Oh, how the wind does blow.
It stings the toes and bites the nose
As over the ground we go.

Over the river and through the woods
To have a full day of play.
Oh, hear the bells ringing ting-a-ling-ling,
For it is Christmas Day.
Over the river and through the woods,
Trot fast my dapple gray;
Spring o'er the ground just like a hound,
For this is Christmas Day.

Over the river and through the woods
And straight through the barnyard gate.
It seems that we go so dreadfully slow;
It is so hard to wait.
Over the river and through the woods,
Now Grandma's cap I spy.
Hurrah for fun; the pudding's done;
Hurrah for the pumpkin pie.

Winter Wonderland

Words by Dick Smith; Music by Felix Bernard

Sleighbells ring, are you list'nin'?
In the lane, snow is glist'nin',
A beautiful sight, we're happy tonight,
Walkin' in a winter wonderland!
Gone away is the bluebird,
Here to stay is a new bird,
He sings a love song, as we go along,
Walkin' in a winter wonderland!

In the meadow we can build a snowman,
Then pretend that he is Parson Brown;
He'll say, "Are you married?"
We'll say, "No, man!
But you can do the job when you're in town!"
Later on, we'll conspire,
As we dream by the fire,
To face unafraid, the plans that we made,
Walkin' in a winter wonderland!
Yes! Walkin' in a winter wonderland!

Jingle-Bell Rock

Words and Music by Joe Beal and Jim Boothe

Jingle-bell, jingle-bell, jingle-bell rock,
Jingle bells swing and jingle bells ring.
Snowin' and blowin' up bushels of fun,
Now the jingle hop has begun.
Jingle-bell, jingle-bell, jingle-bell rock,
Jingle bells chime in jingle-bell time.
Dancin' and prancin' in Jingle Bell Square
In the frosty air.
What a bright time; it's the right time
To rock the night away.
Jingle-bell time is a swell time
To go glidin' in a one-horse sleigh.
Giddy-yap jingle horse; pick up your feet;
Jingle around the clock.
Mix and mingle in a jinglin' beat;
That's the jingle-bell rock.

Winter

Words by Alfred Bryan; Music by Albert Gumble

Winter, winter,
When the snow is softly falling,
That's the time to squeeze, when it starts to freeze.
In October and November and December, just remember
Winter, winter,
When your sweetheart comes a-calling,
By the fireside so bright, you'll sit and tease her;
That's the time to squeeze her, when it's winter.

Jing-A-Ling, Jing-A-Ling

Words by Don Raye; Music by Paul J. Smith

Jing, jing-a-ling, jing-a-ling, jing-a-ling,
What fun to hear the sleigh bells jingle.
Jing, jing-a-ling, jing-a-ling, jing-a-ling,
They set your heart atingle.
Jing, jing-a-ling, jing-a-ling, jing-a-ling,
I love to hear our laughter mingle,
Ha, ha, ho, ho, through the snow we go.

Jing, jing-a-ling, jing-a-ling, jing-a-ling,
The bells have got the snowflakes dancing.
Jing, jing-a-ling, jing-a-ling, jing-a-ling,
Ol' Dobbin's even prancing.
Jing, jing-a-ling, jing-a-ling, jing-a-ling,
The night is made for sweet romancing.
Ha, ha, ho, ho, through the snow we go.

Through a winter fairyland we go a-gliding
In a cotton-candy land of frozen charms,
And the way the sleigh is slipping and a-sliding
Brings you sliding even closer in my arms.
Can't you hear the sleigh bells asking why we're single,
As we fly across the snowy hills and dells?
And we're happy 'cause the sleigh bells seem to jingle
In the winter fairyland like wedding bells.

REPEAT FIRST TWO VERSES
Jing, jing-a-ling, jing-a-ling, jing-a-ling, jing-a-ling,
   jing-a-ling, jing-a-ling.

SECTION 5
Modern Carols

Out of the East

Words and Music by Harry Noble

Out of the East there came riding, riding,
Three of the wisest of men.
Dust was their enemy blinding, blinding,
Even the wisest of them.
Wandering shepherds heard tell their story,
Told in the flickering firelight, tender light, ever bright
   Christmas night.
Far to the West was there shining, shining,
Blazing a star in the dawn;

Reverent wise men beheld it, saying,
"This night a Savior is born."

Into the West they went riding, riding,
Following after the star,
Over a quiet town shining, shining,
Lighting their way from afar.
Under its glory sat Mother Mary
Tenderly singing a lullaby, hush-a-by, don't-you-cry lullaby.
Into the stable came riding, riding,
Three of the wisest of men;
Gifts did they bring for that Babe in manger,
Gifts for the Savior of men.

Lo! in a manger they found Him, found Him,
Bathed in the light of yon star;
Gold did they bring Him and frankincense,
And myrrh from a land that was far.
Shepherds crept in singing praises, praises;
Angels kept watch to be near to Him, dear to Him, one with
    Him, praising Him.
Into the East then went riding, riding,
Three of the wisest of men.
Found was the Babe in a lowly manger,
Crowned was the Savior of men.

I Heard the Bells on Christmas Day

*Words by Henry Wadsworth Longfellow, adapted
by Johnny Marks; Music by Johnny Marks*

I heard the bells on Christmas Day
Their old familiar carols play,
And wild and sweet the words repeat
Of peace on earth, goodwill to men.

I thought as now this day had come,
The belfries of all Christendom
Had rung so long the unbroken song
Of peace on earth, goodwill to men

And in despair I bowed my head;
"There is no peace on earth," I said,
"For hate is strong and mocks the song
Of peace on earth, goodwill to men."

Then pealed the bells more loud and deep:
"God is not dead, nor doth He sleep;
The wrong shall fail, the right prevail
With peace on earth, goodwill to men."

The Little Drummer Boy

*Words and Music by Katherine Davis,
Henry Onorati and Harry Simeone*

Come, they told me,
(Pa-rum-pum-pum-pum)
A newborn King to see;
(Pa-rum-pum-pum-pum)
Our finest gifts we bring
(Pa-rum-pum-pum-pum)
To lay before the King,
(Pa-rum-pum-pum-pum, rum-pum-pum-pum,
    rum-pum-pum-pum)
So to honor Him
(Pa-rum-pum-pum-pum)
When we come.

Little Baby *[Baby Gesu]*,
(Pa-rum-pum-pum-pum)
I am a poor boy too;
(Pa-rum-pum-pum-pum)
I have no gift to bring
(Pa-rum-pum-pum-pum)
That's fit to give our King.
(Pa-rum-pum-pum-pum, rum-pum-pum-pum,
    rum-pum-pum-pum)
Shall I play for You
(Pa-rum-pum-pum-pum)
On my drum?

Mary nodded;
(Pa-rum-pum-pum-pum)
The ox and lamb kept time;
(Pa-rum-pum-pum-pum)
I played my drum for Him;
(Pa-rum-pum-pum-pum)
I played my best for Him.
(Pa-rum-pum-pum-pum, rum-pum-pum-pum,
    rum-pum-pum-pum)
Then He smiled at me,
(Pa-rum-pum-pum-pum)
Me and my drum.

Carol of the Bells

Words by Peter J. Wilhousky; Music by M. Leontovich

Hark! how the bells,
Sweet silver bells,
All seem to say,
"Throw cares away."
Christmas is here,
Bringing good cheer
To young and old,
Meek and the bold.

(continued on next page)

Ding, dong, ding, dong,
That is their song
With joyful ring,
All caroling.
One seems to hear
Words of good cheer
From ev'rywhere
Filling the air;
O how happy are their tones.
Gaily they ring
While people sing
Songs of good cheer,
Christmas is here;
Merry, merry, merry, merry Christmas,
Merry, merry, merry, merry Christmas,
On, on they send,
On without end,
Their joyful tone
To ev'ry home.

REPEAT FROM BEGINNING
On, on they send,
On without end,
Their joyful tone
To ev'ry home.
Ding, dong, ding, dong.

The Peace Carol

Words and Music by Bob Beers

The garment of life be it tattered and torn,
The cloak of the soldier is weathered and worn,
But what Child is this that was poverty-born?
The peace of Christmas Day.

CHORUS
The branch that bears the bright holly,
The dove that rests in yonder tree,
The light that shines for all to see,
The peace of Christmas Day.

The hope that has slumbered for two thousand years,
A promise that silenced a thousand fears,
A faith that can hobble an ocean of tears,
The peace of Christmas Day.
CHORUS

Add all the grief that people may bear;
Total the strife and the trouble and care;
Put them in columns and leave them right there,
The peace of Christmas Day.
CHORUS

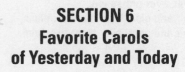

SECTION 6
Favorite Carols
of Yesterday and Today

I Saw Three Ships

Traditional

I saw three ships come sailing in
On Christmas Day, on Christmas Day.
I saw three ships come sailing in
On Christmas Day in the morning.
And what was in those ships all three
On Christmas Day, on Christmas Day?
And what was in those ships all three
On Christmas Day in the morning?
The Virgin Mary and Christ were there
On Christmas Day, on Christmas Day;
The Virgin Mary and Christ were there
On Christmas Day in the morning.

O Holy Night

Words by John Sullivan Dwight; Music by Adolphe Charles Adam

O holy night, the stars are brightly shining;
It is the night of the dear Savior's birth.
Long lay the world in sin and error pining,
Till He appeared and the soul felt its worth.
A thrill of hope, the weary soul rejoices,.
For yonder breaks a new and glorious morn.
Fall on your knees,
Oh, hear the angel voices!
O night divine, O night when Christ was born!
O night, O holy night, O night divine!

Led by the light of faith serenely beaming,
With glowing hearts by His cradle we stand.
So led by light of a star sweetly gleaming,
Here came the wise men from the Orient land.
The King of Kings lay in lowly manger,
In all our trials born to be our friend.
He knows our need,
To our weakness no stranger.
Behold your King! before the lowly bend!
Behold your King! your King! before Him bend!

Truly He taught us to love one another;
His law is love and His gospel is peace.
Chains shall He break, for the slave is our brother,
And in His name all oppression shall cease.
Sweet hymns of joy in grateful chorus rise we,

Let all within us praise His holy name.
Christ is the Lord,
Then ever, ever praise we;
His pow'r and glory ever more proclaim,
His pow'r and glory ever more proclaim.

Angels from the Realms of Glory

Words by James Montgomery; Music by Henry Smart

Angels from the realms of glory
Wing your flight o'er all the earth.
Ye who sang creation's story
Now proclaim Messiah's birth.

CHORUS
Come and worship, come and worship;
Worship Christ, the newborn King.

Shepherds in the fields abiding,
Watching o'er your flocks by night.
God with man is now residing;
Yonder shines the infant Light.
CHORUS

Sages, leave your contemplations;
Brighter visions beam afar.
Seek the great desire of nations;
Ye have seen Him natal star.
CHORUS

Saints before the altar bending,
Watching long in hope and fear.
Suddenly the Lord descending
In His temple shall appear.
CHORUS

Lo, How a Rose E'er Blooming

Traditional; Arranged by Dan Fox

Lo, how a rose e'er blooming
From tender stem hath sprung,
Of Jesse's lineage coming,
As men of old have sung.
It came a floweret bright
Amid the cold of winter,
When half spent was the night.
Isaiah 'twas foretold it,
The rose I have in mind.
With Mary we behold it,
The Virgin Mother kind.
To show God's love aright,
She bore to men a Savior
When half spent was the night.

Copyright © 1981 by Robbins Music Corporation.

Joseph Dearest, Joseph Mild

Traditional

Joseph dearest, Joseph mild,
Help me rock my little Child.
God will give you your reward in heav'n above,
The Son of Virgin Mary.

Gladly, dearest, Mary mine,
I will rock your Kindelein.
God will give me my reward in heav'n above,
The Child of Virgin Mary.

Lulla, lulla, lullaby,
(Hum music for this line)
Lulla, lulla, lullaby *(Hum music to end of line)*
The Son of Virgin Mary.

Christians, Awake, Salute the Happy Morn

Words by John Byrom; Music by John Wainwright

Christians, awake, salute the happy morn
Whereon the Savior of the world was born.
Rise to adore the mystery of love
Which hosts of angels chanted from above,
With them the joyful tidings first begun
Of God incarnate and the Virgin's Son.

Then to the watchful shepherds it was told,
Who heard the angelic herald's voice: "Behold,
I bring good tidings of a Savior's birth
To you and all the nations upon earth.
This day hath God fulfilled His promised word;
This day is born a Savior, Christ the Lord."

He spake, and straightaway the celestial choir,
In hymns of joy, unknown before, conspire;
The praises of redeeming love they sang,
And heaven's whole orb with alleluias rang.
God's highest glory was their anthem still,
Peace upon earth and unto men goodwill.

To Bethlehem straight the shepherds ran
To see the wonder God had wrought for man,
And found, with Joseph and the blessed Maid,
Her Son, the Savior, in a manger laid.
Amazed, the wondrous story they proclaim,
The earliest heralds of the Savior's name.

Let us, like these good shepherds, then employ
Our grateful voices to proclaim the joy.
Trace we the Babe, who hath retrieved our loss,
From His poor manger to His bitter cross,
Treading His steps, assisted by His grace,
Till man's first heavenly state again takes place.

(continued on next page)

Then may we hope, the angelic thrones among,
To sing, redeemed, a glad triumphal song.
He that was born upon this joyful day
Around us all His glory shall display.
Saved by His love, incessant we shall sing
Of angels and of angel-men the King.

The Holly and the Ivy

Traditional

The holly and the ivy,
When they are both full grown,
Of all the trees that are in the wood,
The holly bears the crown.

CHORUS
The rising of the sun
And the running of the deer,
The playing of the merry organ,
Sweet singing in the choir.

The holly bears a blossom
As white as lily flow'r,
And Mary bore sweet Jesus Christ
To be our sweet Savior.
CHORUS

The holly bears a berry
As red as any blood,
And Mary bore sweet Jesus Christ
To do poor sinners good.
CHORUS

As Lately We Watched

Traditional

As lately we watched o'er our fields through the night,
A star there was seen of such glorious light.
All through the night angels did sing,
In carols so sweet of the birth of a King.

His throne is a manger, His court is a loft,
But troops of bright angels in lays sweet and soft,
Him they proclaim, our Christ by name,
And earth and sky and air straight are filled with his fame.

Then shepherds be joyful, salute your new King;
Let hills and dales ring to the song that ye sing.
Blessed be the hour, welcome the morn,
For Christ our dear Savior on earth now is born.

What Child Is This?

Words by William Chatterton Dix; Music Traditional

What Child is this, who laid to rest,
On Mary's lap is sleeping?
Whom angels greet with anthems sweet
While shepherds watch are keeping?

CHORUS
This, this is Christ the King,
Whom shepherds guard and angels sing.
Haste, haste to bring Him laud,
The Babe, the Son of Mary.

Why lies He in such mean estate
Where ox and ass are feeding?
Good Christian, fear for sinners here,
The silent Word is pleading.
CHORUS

So bring Him incense, gold and myrrh;
Come, peasant king, to own Him.
The King of Kings salvation brings;
Let loving hearts enthrone Him.
CHORUS

Good Christian Men, Rejoice

Words by John Mason Neale; Music Traditional

Good Christian men, rejoice
With heart and soul and voice.
Give ye heed to what we say;
News! News!
Jesus Christ is born today.
Ox and ass before Him bow,
And He is in the manger now.
Christ is born today!
Christ is born today!

Good Christian men, rejoice
With heart and soul and voice.
Now ye hear of endless bliss:
Joy! Joy!
Jesus Christ was born for this.
He hath ope'd the heav'nly door,
And man is blessed evermore.
Christ was born for this;
Christ was born for this.

Good Christian men, rejoice
With heart and soul and voice.
Now ye need not fear the grave:
Peace! Peace!

Jesus Christ was born to save.
Calls you one and calls you all
To gain His everlasting hall.
Christ was born to save;
Christ was born to save.

Once in Royal David's City

Words by Mrs. C. F. Alexander; Music by H. J. Gauntlett

Once in royal David's city
Stood a lowly cattle shed,
Where a mother laid her Baby
In a manger for His bed.
Mary was that mother mild,
Jesus Christ her little Child.

He came down to earth from heaven,
Who is God and Lord of all,
And His shelter was a stable,
And His cradle was a stall.
With the poor and mean and lowly
Lived on earth our Savior holy.

And our eyes at last shall see Him
Through His own redeeming love,
For that Child so dear and gentle
Is our Lord in heaven above.
And He leads His children on
To the place where He is gone.

✳✳✳✳✳

O Come, O Come Emmanuel

Traditional

O come, O come Emmanuel
And ransom captive Israel
That mourns in lonely exile here
Until the Son of God appear.

CHORUS
Rejoice! Rejoice! Emmanuel
Shall come to thee O Israel.

O Come, Thou Rod of Jesse, free
Thine own from Satan's tyranny.
From depths of Hell Thy people save,
And give them vict'ry o'er the grave.
CHORUS

O come, O Day-spring come and cheer
Our spirits by Thine advent here,
And drive away the shades of night,
And pierce the clouds and bring us light.
CHORUS

While Shepherds Watched Their Flocks by Night

*Words by Nahum Tate and Nicholas Brody;
Music by George Frederick Handel*

While shepherds watched their flocks by night,
All seated on the ground,
The angel of the Lord came down,
And glory shone around,
And glory shone around.

"Fear not," he said, for mighty dread
Had seized their troubled minds.
"Glad tidings of great joy I bring
To you and all mankind,
To you and all mankind."

"To you in David's town this day
Is born of David's line,
The Savior who is Christ the Lord,
And this shall be the sign,
And this shall be the sign."

"The heavenly Babe you there shall find
To human view displayed,
And meanly wrapped in swathing bands,
And in a manger laid,
And in a manger laid."

Thus spake the seraph, and forthwith
Appeared a shining throng
Of angels praising God, who thus
Addressed their joyful song,
Addressed their joyful song.

"All glory be to God on high,
And to the earth be peace;
Goodwill henceforth from heaven to men
Begin and never cease,
Begin and never cease!"

As with Gladness Men of Old

Words by William Chatterton Dix; Music by Conrad Kocher

As with gladness men of old
Did the guiding star behold.
As with joy they hailed its light,
Leading onward, beaming bright.
So most gracious God may we
Evermore be led by Thee.

As with joyful steps they sped
To that lowly manger bed,
There to bend the knee before
Him whom heav'n and earth adore;
So may we with willing feet
Ever seek Thy mercy seat.

22

(continued on next page)

As they offered gifts most rare
At that manger rude and bare,
So may we with holy joy,
Pure and free from sin's alloy,
All our costliest treasures bring
Christ to Thee, our heav'nly King.

Holy Jesus ev'ry day
Keep us in the narrow way,
And when earthly things are past,
Bring our ransomed souls at last
Where they need no star to guide,
Where no clouds Thy glory hide.

SECTION 7
Christmas
Round the World

Bring a Torch, Jeannette, Isabella

Traditional

Bring a torch, Jeannette, Isabella;
Bring a torch, come swiftly and run.
Christ is born tell the folk of the village;
Jesus is sleeping in his cradle.
Ah, ah, beautiful is the Mother;
Ah, ah, beautiful is her Son.

Hasten now, good folk of the village;
Hasten now, the Christ-Child to see.
You will find him asleep in the manger;
Quietly come and whisper softly,
Hush, hush, peacefully now He slumbers;
Hush, hush, peacefully now He sleeps.

Mele Kalikimaka
(The Hawaiian Christmas Song)

Words and Music by R. Alex Anderson

Mele Kalikimaka is the thing to say
On a bright Hawaiian Christmas Day.
That's the island greeting that we send to you
From the land where palm trees sway.
Here we know that Christmas will be green and bright,
The sun to shine by day and all the stars at night.
Mele Kalikimaka is Hawaii's way
To say "Merry Christmas to you."

The Coventry Carol

Traditional

Lullay, Thou little tiny Child,
Bye-bye, lulloo, lullay.
Lullay, Thou little tiny Child,
Bye-bye, lulloo, lullay.

O sisters, too, how may we do
For to preserve this day?
This poor Youngling for whom we sing,
Bye-bye, lulloo, lullay.

Herod the king in his raging
Charged he hath this day
His men of might, in his own sight,
All children young to slay.

Then woe is me, poor Child for Thee,
And ever morn and day,
For Thy parting nor say nor sing,
Bye-bye, lulloo, lullay.

O Sanctissima

Traditional

O thou happy,
O thou holy,
Glorious peace bringing Christmastime.
Angel throngs to meet thee;
On Thy birth we greet thee;
All hail Jesus, our Savior King.
Day of holiness,
Peace and happiness,
Joyful, glorious Christmas Day.
Angels tell the story
Of this day of glory;
Praise Christ, our Savior, born this Christmas Day.

O Come, Little Children

Words and Music by Christoph von Schmidt and J. A. P. Schulz

O come, little children, from cot and from hall;
O come to the manger in Bethlehem's stall.
There meekly He lieth, the heavenly Child,
So poor and so humble, so sweet and so mild.

The hay is His pillow, the manger His bed;
The beasts stand in wonder to gaze on His head.
Yet there where He lieth, so weak and so poor,
Come shepherds and wise men to kneel at His door.

Now "Glory to God" sing the angels on high,
"And peace upon earth" heav'nly voices reply.

Then come, little children, and join in the lay
That gladdened the world on that first Christmas Day.

The Friendly Beasts

Traditional

Jesus our brother, kind and good,
Was humbly born in a stable rude,
And the friendly beasts around Him stood,
Jesus our brother, kind and good.

"I," said the donkey, shaggy and brown,
"I carried His mother up hill and down;
I carried her safely to Bethlehem town."
"I," said the donkey, shaggy and brown.

"I," said the cow, all white and red,
"I gave Him my manger for a bed;
I gave Him my hay to pillow His head."
"I," said the cow, all white and red.

"I," said the sheep with curly horn,
"I gave Him my wool for His blanket warm;
He wore my coat on Christmas morn."
"I," said the sheep with curly horn.

"I," said the dove from the rafters high,
"Cooed Him to sleep that He should not cry;
We cooed Him to sleep, my mate and I."
"I," said the dove from the rafters high.

"I," said the camel, yellow and black,
"Over the desert, upon my back,
I brought Him a gift in the Wise Men's pack."
"I," said the camel, yellow and black.

Thus every beast by some good spell,
In the stable dark was glad to tell
Of the gift he gave Emmanuel,
The gift he gave Emmanuel.

Hey, Ho, Nobody Home

Traditional; Arranged by Dan Fox
(Sung As a Round)

Voice 1   Hey, ho, nobody home;
Voice 1 ⎱ Meat nor drink nor money have I none,
Voice 2 ⎰ Hey, ho, nobody home;
Voice 1 ⎱ Yet will I be merry.
Voice 2 ⎰ Meat nor drink nor money have I none,
Voice 3 ⎱ Hey, ho, nobody home;
Voice 1 ⎰ Hey, ho, nobody home;
Voice 2 ⎱ Yet will I be merry.
Voice 3 ⎰ Meat nor drink nor money have I none,
Voice 1 ⎱ Meat nor drink nor money have I none,
Voice 3 ⎰ Yet will I be merry.
Voice 1   Yet will I be merry.

'Twas in the Moon of Wintertime
(The Huron Christmas Carol)

English words by J. E. Middleton;
Original Huron words by Father Jean de Brébeuf;
Music Traditional

'Twas in the moon of wintertime when all the birds had fled
That mighty Gitchi Manitou sent angel choirs instead.
Before their light the stars grew dim, and wond'ring hunters
    heard the hymn:

CHORUS
Jesus, your King, is born;
Jesus is born!
In excelsis gloria!

Within a lodge of broken bark, the tender Babe was
    found;
A ragged robe of rabbit skin enwrapped His beauty
    round.
And as the hunter braves drew nigh, the angel song rang
    loud and high:
CHORUS

O children of the forest free, O sons of Manitou,
The Holy Child of earth and heav'n is born today for you.
Come kneel before the radiant Boy who brings you
    beauty, peace and joy:
CHORUS

STANZA 1 IN HURON
Estennialon de tsonoue
Jesous ahatonhia
Onnaouateoua d'oki
N'onouandaskouaentak
Ennonchien skouatrihotat
N'onouandilonrachatha
Jesous ahatonhia.

Burgundian Carol

French Carol; English lyrics and
Music adaptation by Oscar Brand

The winter season of the year
When to this world our Lord was born,
The ox and donkey, so they say,
Did keep His holy presence warm.
How many oxen and donkeys now,
If they were there when first He came,
How many oxen and donkeys you know,
At such a time would do the same?

And on that night it has been told
These humble beasts so rough and rude,

                                    (continued on next page)

Throughout the night of holy birth,
Drank no water, ate no food.
How many oxen and donkeys now,
Dressed in ermine, silk and such,
How many oxen and donkeys you know,
At such a time would do as much?

As soon as to these humble beasts
Appeared our Lord so mild and sweet,
With joy they knelt before His grace,
And gently kissed His tiny feet.
If we, like oxen and donkeys then,
In spite of all the things we've heard,
Would be like oxen and donkeys then,
We'd hear the truth, believe His word.

All Hail to Thee

Words by Ernest W. Olson; Music by Philipp Nicolai

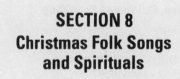

All hail to thee O blessed morn,
To tidings long by prophets borne.
Hast thou fulfillment given,
O sacred and immortal day,
When unto earth in glorious ray
Descends the grace of heaven,
Young and old, their voices blending,
Praise are sending unto heaven
For the Savior to us given.

He comes for our redemption sent,
And by His glory heav'n is rent
To close upon us never;
Our blessed Shepherd He would be,
Whom we may follow faithfully.
To live with Him forever
Unto realms of glory winging
Praises, singing to the Father and the
Son and Spirit ever.

Buon Natale (Merry Christmas to You)

Words and Music by Bob Saffer and Frank Linale

Buon Natale means "Merry Christmas to you."
Buon Natale to ev'ryone,
Happy New Year and lots of fun.
Buon Natale, may all your wishes come true.
Buon Natale in Italy means a "Merry Christmas to you."
Far away across the sea
In sunny Italy,
There's a quaint little town,
Not a clock has been wound for over a century.

They don't know the time or year,
And no one seems to care,
And this is the reason the Christmas season
is celebrated all year.

REPEAT FIRST FIVE LINES

Pat-A-Pan

Traditional

Willie, take your little drum;
Robin, take your flute and come.
When we hear the tune you play
Tu-re-lu-re-lu, pat-a-pat-a-pan;
When we hear the tune you play,
How can anyone be glum?

When the men of olden days
Gave the King of Kings their praise,
They had pipes on which to play
Tu-re-lu-re-lu, pat-a-pat-a-pan.
They had drums on which to play,
Full of joy on Christmas Day.

God and man this day become
Joined as one with flute and drum.
Let the happy tune play on
Tu-re-lu-re-lu, pat-a-pat-a-pan.
Flute and drum together play
As we sing on Christmas Day.

SECTION 8
Christmas Folk Songs and Spirituals

Go Tell It on the Mountain

Traditional

When I was a sinner,
I prayed both night and day;
I asked the Lord to aid me,
And He showed me the way:

CHORUS
Go tell it on the mountain,
Over the hills and ev'rywhere;

Go tell it on the mountain,
Our Jesus Christ is born.

When I was a seeker,
I sought both night and day;
I asked the Lord to help me,
And He taught me how to pray.
CHORUS

Down in a lowly manger
The humble Christ was born;
And God sent out salvation
That blessed Christmas morn.
CHORUS

I Wonder As I Wander

Words and Music by John Jacob Niles

I wonder as I wander out under the sky
How Jesus the Savior did come for to die.
For poor on'ry people like you and like I;
I wonder as I wander out under the sky.

When Mary birthed Jesus, 'twas in a cow's stall,
With wise men and farmers and shepherds and all.
But high from God's heaven, a star's light did fall,
And the promise of ages it then did recall.

If Jesus had wanted for any wee thing,
A star in the sky or a bird on the wing,
Or all of God's angels in heav'n for to sing,
He surely could have it, 'cause He was the King.

REPEAT VERSE 1

Children, Go Where I Send Thee

Traditional

Children, go where I send thee.
How shall I send thee?
I'm gonna send thee one by one;
One's for the little itty Baby,
Born, born Lord,
Born in Bethlehem.

Children, go where I send thee.
How shall I send thee?
I'm gonna send thee two by two, 'cause
Two was a Paul and Silas, and
One was the little itty Baby,
Born, born Lord,
Born in Bethlehem.

Children, go where I send thee.
How shall I send thee?
I'm gonna send thee three by three, 'cause

Three was the Hebrew children, and
Two was a Paul and Silas, and
One was the little itty Baby,
Born, born Lord,
Born in Bethlehem.

Children, go where I send thee.
How shall I send thee?
I'm gonna send thee four by four, 'cause
Four was the poor came knockin' on the door, and
Three was the Hebrew children, and
Two was a Paul and Silas, and
One was the little itty Baby,
Born, born Lord,
Born in Bethlehem.

Children, go where I send thee.
How shall I send thee?
I'm gonna send thee five by five, 'cause
Five was the gospel preachers, and
Four was the poor came knockin' on the door, and
Three was the Hebrew children, and
Two was a Paul and Silas, and
One was the little itty Baby,
Born, born Lord,
Born in Bethlehem.

Children, go where I send thee.
How shall I send thee?
I'm gonna send thee six by six,
Six for the six that couldn't be fixed, and
Five was the gospel preachers, and
Four was the poor came knockin' on the door, and
Three was the Hebrew children, and
Two was a Paul and Silas, and
One was the little itty Baby,
Born, born Lord,
Born in Bethlehem.

Children, go where I send thee.
How shall I send thee?
I'm gonna send thee seven by seven,
Seven for the seven that went up to heaven, and
Six for the six that couldn't be fixed, and
Five was the gospel preachers, and
Four was the poor came knockin' on the door, and
Three was the Hebrew children, and
Two was a Paul and Silas, and
One was the little itty Baby,
Born, born Lord,
Born in Bethlehem.

Children, go where I send thee.
How shall I send thee?
I'm gonna send thee eight by eight,
Eight for the eight that stood at the gate, and
Seven for the seven that went up to heaven, and
Six for the six that couldn't be fixed, and
Five was the gospel preachers, and
Four was the poor came knockin' on the door, and

(continued on next page)

Three was the Hebrew children, and
Two was a Paul and Silas, and
One was the little itty Baby,
Born, born Lord,
Born in Bethlehem.

Children, go where I send thee.
How shall I send thee?
I'm gonna send thee nine by nine,
Nine for the nine that got left behind, and
Eight for the eight that stood at the gate, and
Seven for the seven that went up to heaven, and
Six for the six that couldn't be fixed, and
Five was the gospel preachers, and
Four was the poor came knockin' on the door, and
Three was the Hebrew children, and
Two was a Paul and Silas, and
One was the little itty Baby,
Born, born Lord,
Born in Bethlehem.

Children, go where I send thee.
How shall I send thee?
I'm gonna send thee ten by ten,
Ten for the Ten Commandments, and
Nine for the nine that got left behind, and
Eight for the eight that stood at the gate, and
Seven for the seven that went up to heaven, and
Six for the six that couldn't be fixed, and
Five was the gospel preachers, and
Four was the poor came knockin' on the door, and
Three was the Hebrew children, and
Two was a Paul and Silas, and
One was the little itty Baby,
Born, born Lord,
Born in Bethlehem.

Rise Up, Shepherd, and Follow

Traditional

There's a star in the East on Christmas morn;
Rise up, shepherd, and follow.
It will lead to the place where the Savior's born;
Rise up, shepherd, and follow.

CHORUS
Follow, follow,
Rise up, shepherd, and follow;
Follow the star of Bethlehem;
Rise up, shepherd, and follow.

If you take good heed to the angel's words,
Rise up, shepherd, and follow.
You'll forget your flocks; you'll forget your herds;
Rise up, shepherd, and follow.
CHORUS

Sweet Little Jesus Boy

Words and Music by Robert MacGimsey

Sweet little Jesus Boy,
They made You be born in a manguh (manger).
Sweet little Holy Chil',
Didn't know who You wus (was).
Didn't know You'd come to save us Lawd,
To take our sins away.
Our eyes wus bline (was blind);
We couldn't see;
We didn't know who You wus (was).
Long time ago You wus bawn (was born),
Bawn in a manguh (manger) low,
Sweet little Jesus Boy.
De worl' (the world) treat You mean Lawd,
Treat me mean too,
But please, Suh, fuhgive (Sir, forgive) us Lawd;
We didn't know 'twas You,
Sweet little Jesus Boy.
Bawn (born) long time ago,
Sweet little Holy chil',
An' we didn't know who You wus (was).

SECTION 9
Christmas Classics and Instrumental Favorites

Parade of the Wooden Soldiers

Words by Ballard Macdonald; Music by Leon Jessel

The toy shop door is locked up tight,
And ev'rything is quiet for the night.
When suddenly the clock strikes twelve,
The fun's begun.
The dolls are in their best arrayed;
There's going to be a wonderful parade.
Hark to the drum, oh, here they come,
Cries ev'ryone.
Hear them all cheering,
Now they are nearing;
There's the captain stiff as starch.
Bayonets flashing,
Music is crashing
As the wooden soldiers march.
Sabers a-clinking,
Soldiers a-winking
At each pretty little maid.
Here they come,
Here they come,
Here they come,
Here they come,
Wooden solders on parade.

March of the Kings

Traditional; Arranged by Noble Cain

Three great kings I met at early morn,
With all their retinue were slowly marching.
Three great kings I met at early morn
Were on their way to meet the newly born,
With gifts of gold brought from far away
And valiant warriors to guard the royal treasure;
With gifts of gold brought from far away,
Their shields all shining in their bright array.

Ce matin, j'ai rencontré le train
De trois grands rois qui allaient en voyage.
Ce matin, j'ai rencontré le train
De trois grands rois dessus le grand chemin,
Tout chargés d'or les suivaient d'abord,
De grands guerriers et les gardes du trésor;
Tout chargés d'or les suivaient d'abord;
De grands guerriers avec leurs boucliers.

The Virgin's Slumber Song

English words by Edward Teschemacher; Music by Max Reger

Amid the roses Mary sits and rocks her Jesus-Child,
While amid the treetops sighs the breeze so warm and mild,
And soft and sweetly sings a bird upon the bough,
Ah, Baby, dear one,
Slumber now.
Happy is Thy laughter; holy is Thy silent rest.
Lay Thy head in slumber fondly on Thy mother's breast.
Ah, Baby, dear one,
Slumber now.

Break Forth, O Beauteous, Heavenly Light

*Words and Music by Johann Rist and Johann Schop;
Harmonized by Johann Sebastian Bach*

Break forth, O beauteous, heav'nly light
And usher in the morning.
Ye shepherds, shrink not with affright,
But hear the angel's warning.
This Child now weak in infancy
Our confidence and joy shall be;
The pow'r of Satan breaking,
Our peace eternal making.

SECTION 10
Ring Out the Old!
Ring In the New Year!

For Thy Mercy and Thy Grace

Words by Henry Downton;
Music by Georg Christoph Strattner

For Thy mercy and Thy grace,
Constant through another year,
Hear our song of thankfulness,
Father and Redeemer hear.

Dark the future; let Thy light
Guide us, bright and morning star.
Fierce our foes and hard the fight,
Arm us Savior for the war.

In our weakness and distress,
Rock of strength be Thou our stay;
In the pathless wilderness,
Be our true and living way.

Keep us faithful; keep us pure;
Keep us evermore Thine own.
Help, O help us to endure;
Fit us for the promised crown.

Ring Out, Wild Bells

Words by Alfred, Lord Tennyson;
Music Traditional

Ring out, wild bells, to the wild sky,
Thy flying cloud, the frosty light.
The year is dying in the night;
Ring out, wild bells, and let him die.

Ring out the old, ring in the new;
Ring, happy bells, across the snow.
The year is going, let him go;
Ring out the false, ring in the true.

Ring out false pride in place and blood,
The civic slander and the spite;
Ring in the love of truth and right;
Ring in the common love of good.

Ring in the valiant man and free,
The larger heart, the kindlier hand;
Ring out the darkness of the land;
Ring in the Christ that is to be.

What Are You Doing New Year's Eve

Words and Music by Frank Loesser

Maybe it's much too early in the game,
Ah, but I thought I'd ask you just the same,
"What are you doing New Year's, New Year's Eve?"
Wonder whose arms will hold you good and tight,
When it's exactly twelve o'clock that night,
Welcoming in the New Year's, New Year's Eve.
Maybe I'm crazy to suppose
I'd ever be the one you chose
Out of the thousand invitations you'll receive.
Ah, but in case I stand one little chance,
Here comes the jackpot question in advance,
"What are you doing New Year's, New Year's Eve?"

Auld Lang Syne

Words by Robert Burns; Music Traditional

Should auld acquaintance be forgot
And never brought to mind?
Should auld acquaintance be forgot
And days of Auld Lang Syne?
For Auld Lang Syne, my dear,
For Auld Lang Syne;
We'll take a cup of kindness yet
For Auld Lang Syne.

And here's a hand, my trusty friend,
And gives a hand o' thine;
We'll take a cup o' kindness yet
For Auld Lang Syne.

Reader's Digest publishes other music products. *Remembering Yesterday's Hits, Treasury of Great Show Tunes, Celebration of Christmas,* and *Children's Songbook.* You can order the books by calling the Reader's Digest toll-free customer number 1-800-846-2100. The contents of several of these books are listed below and on the following page.

THE READER'S DIGEST CHILDREN'S SONGBOOK

Actor's Life for Me, An (Hi-Diddle-Dee-Dee)
Alley Cat Song, The
Alouette
Alphabet Song, The
Animal Fair, The
A-Tisket A-Tasket
Baa, Baa, Black Sheep
Barney Google
Be Kind to Your Web-Footed Friends
Billy Boy
Bingo
Bunny Hop, The
Camptown Races
Casper the Friendly Ghost
Cement Mixer (Put-ti, Put-ti)
Chickery Chick
Clementine
Cockles and Mussels
Comin' Thru the Rye
Ding-Dong! the Witch Is Dead
Do-Re-Mi
Down by the Station
Dwarfs' Marching Song, The ("Heigh-Ho")
Dwarfs' Yodel Song, The (The Silly Song)
Eensy, Weensy Spider
Farmer in the Dell, The
Father's Old Grey Whiskers
Flat Foot Floogee, The
Fox, The
Frère Jacques
Frog Went A-Courtin', A
Frosty the Snow Man
Give a Little Whistle
Going to the Zoo
Green (Bein' Green)
Grey Goose, The
Ha, Ha, This-a-Way
Happy Birthday to You
"Heigh-Ho" (The Dwarfs' Marching Song)
Hey, Diddle, Diddle
Hickory, Dickory, Dock
Hi-Diddle-Dee-Dee (An Actor's Life for Me)
Hokey-Pokey, The
Honor Your Parents
Hot Cross Buns

Humpty Dumpty
Hush, Little Baby
Hut-Sut Song, The
I Know an Old Lady
I Love Little Pussy
I Love Trash
I Whistle a Happy Tune
(I Scream—You Scream—We All Scream for) Ice Cream
If I Only Had a Brain (If I Only Had A Heart) (If I Only Had the Nerve)
If You're Happy and You Know It (Clap Your Hands)
I'm a Little Teapot
I'm Popeye the Sailor Man
Inch Worm, The
It Ain't Gonna Rain No More
I've Been Working on the Railroad
Jack and Jill
John Brown's Baby
John Jacob Jingleheimer Schmidt
Lazy Mary, Will You Get Up?
Little Bo-Peep
Little Boy Blue
Little Brown Jug
Little Jack Horner
Little Miss Muffet
Little White Duck, The
London Bridge
Mail Myself to You
Mairzy Doats
Marianne
Marvelous Toy, The
Me and My Teddy Bear
M-I-S-S-I-S-S-I-P-P-I
Mulberry Bush, The
Muppet Show Theme, The
My Dog's Bigger Than Your Dog
Niña, the Pinta, the Santa María, The
No One Like You
Oats, Peas, Beans and Barley Grow
Oh Where, Oh Where Has My Little Dog Gone?
Old Dan Tucker
Old King Cole
Old MacDonald Had a Farm
On the Good Ship Lollipop
On Top of Spaghetti
One Song
Over the Rainbow

Peter Cottontail
Pink Panther, The
Polly-Wolly-Doodle
Pop! Goes the Weasel
Puff (The Magic Dragon)
Pussy-cat, Pussy-cat
Put Your Finger in the Air
Put Your Little Foot Right Out
Rainbow Connection, The
Remember Your Name and Address
Ride a Cock-horse
Rock-a-Bye Baby
Rock Island Line
Row, Row, Row Your Boat
Rubber Duckie
Rudolph the Red-Nosed Reindeer
Santa Claus Is Comin' to Town
She'll Be Comin' Round the Mountain
Silly Song, The (The Dwarfs' Yodel Song)
Sing!
Sing a Song of Sixpence
Teddy Bears' Picnic, The
Ten Little Indians
(How Much Is) That Doggie in the Window
There Was an Old Woman Who Lived in a Shoe
This Land Is Your Land
This Old Man
Three Blind Mice
Three Little Fishies (Itty Bitty Poo)
Tomorrow
Twinkle, Twinkle, Little Star
Tzena, Tzena, Tzena
Waltzing Matilda
We Gather Together to Ask the Lord's Blessing
We're Off to See the Wizard (The Wonderful Wizard of Oz)
When I See an Elephant Fly
Whistle While You Work
Whistler and His Dog, The
Who's Afraid of the Big Bad Wolf?
Willie the Whistling Giraffe
With a Smile and a Song
Yankee Doodle
Yellow Submarine